Pink Slip to POWERHOUSE
12 Steps to Next

POWERHOUSE QUOTES
for
Powerhouse Thinkers

Pamela R. H. Lue-Hing, BCC

Pink Slip to POWERHOUSE…12 Steps to Next

Email: pamela@pinksliptopowerhouse.com
Website : www.pinksliptopowerhouse.com
LinkedIn : **www.linkedin.com/in/pamelaluehing**
Facebook : www.facebook.com/pamela.luehing
Twitter : @lpstrategist

Legacy Partners Publishing

ISBN-13: 978-0692462737
ISBN-10: 0692462732

DEDICATION

On April 24, 2015 at 7:01 p.m., I bid farewell to a huge part of my life and my existence on this earth was forever changed. My sister, Crystal Faye Flanagan's voice and heartbeat were silenced and she glided into eternal rest.

Crystal knew more about me than anyone in the entire world and was one of my greatest supporters. My best friend kept me going when I wanted to give up. She was my inspiration and the life she lived is now my motivation to do more, give more, love more and become more!

If I can make just half of the positive impact she made on people, I will leave the world a better place. If I learn to see the best in everyone and accept them for who they are as she did, I know I can help more people. If I trust in the Lord the way she did, I know my life will be even more magnificent on this side of Heaven and I will see her again one day!

For every uplifting word she shared with me and for believing in me the way she did, I dedicate this work to her, my sister, my heart, my best friend!!!

I love you Crystal and can truly feel your arms around me…

PREFACE

In today's fast paced society, it is critical to be surrounded with positive people who have the same focus and share the same values. It is even more critical to immerse the mind in ideas that will keep one moving on purpose and to hear and speak words that give life.

Even as a child, I understood this extremely important principle and was always fascinated with how an arrangement of certain words would inspire, encourage, invigorate, stir the soul and shift thought processes.

POWERHOUSE QUOTES for Powerhouse Thinkers is designed with you in mind! It contains a plethora of thought-provoking and intellectually stimulating expressions which will inspire you on your journey as you create your "12 Steps to Next."

Each page contains words of wisdom that will impact the way you think and the decisions you make. It will inspire you to live a life of purpose, focus, intention and gratitude. Most importantly, it will help you become a Powerhouse Thinker!!!

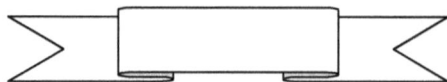

When God activated my gift and gave me freedom to flow, He didn't just turn on a spigot, He ushered in a waterfall.
~ Pamela R. H. Lue-Hing ~

There is a time for everything, and a season for every activity under heaven. ~ Ecclesiastes 3:1 NIV~

Everyone dies. Not everyone really lives.
~ William Wallace~

What happens to a man is less significant than what happens within him. ~ Louis L. Mann ~

If you can't see yourself from the inside, how can others see you from the outside? ~ Dr. Anthony Sanders ~

Teamwork: It is a fact that in the right formation, the lifting power of many wings can achieve twice the distance of any bird flying along. ~ Author Unknown ~

When I go through a crisis I must continue to work. If I don't, two crises will be created: The one I am in and the one that will be created because I didn't continue to work. ~ Liz Kimeria ~

You may not control all the events that happen to you, but you can decide not to be reduced by them. ~ Maya Angelou ~

When God leads you to the edge of the cliff, trust Him fully and let go. Only one of two things will happen: Either He will catch you when you fall or He will teach you how to fly!
~Author unknown ~

Failure is a great teacher, and I think when you make mistakes and you recover from them and you treat them as valuable learning experiences, then you've got something to share.
~ Steve Harvey ~

Before speaking to me about your religion, first show it to me in how you treat other people; Before you tell me how much you love your God, show me how much you love all His children; Before you preach to me of your passion for your faith, teach me about it through your compassion for your neighbors. In the end, I'm not interested in what you have to tell or sell as in how you choose to live and give.
~ Cory Booker, Newark, New Jersey ~

Don't let the darkness from your past block the light of joy in your present. What happened is done. Stop giving time to things which no longer exist, when there is so much joy to be found here and now. ~ Karen Salmansohn (notsalmon.com) ~

And the Lord answered me, and said, 'Write the vision, and make it plain upon tables, that he may run that readeth it'
~ Habakkuk 2:2 ~

Don't sit down and wait for the opportunities to come. Get up and make them! ~ Madam CJ Walker ~

It's easier to build strong children than to repair broken men.
~ Frederick Douglass ~

There comes a time in your life, when you walk away from all the drama and people who create it. You surround yourself with people who make you laugh. Forget the bad, and focus on the good. Love the people who treat you right, pray for the ones who don't. Life is too short to be anything but happy. Falling down is a part of life, getting back up is living." ~ Jose N. Harris~

Entrepreneurship is living a few years of your life like most people won't, so that you can spend the rest of your life like most people can't. ~ Warren G. Tracy's student ~

I've missed more than 9,000 shots in my career. I've lost almost 300 games, 26 times. I've been trusted to take the game winning shot and missed. I've failed over and over and over again in my life. And that is why I succeed. ~ Michael Jordan ~

For I know the plans I have for you, declares the Lord, plans to prosper you and not to harm you, plans to give you hope and a future. Then you will call upon me and come and pray to me, and I will listen to you. You will seek me and find me when you seek me with all your heart. ~ Jeremiah 29:11-13 NIV ~

The first step in the acquisition of wisdom is silence, the second listening, the third memory, the fourth practice, the fifth teaching others. ~ Solomon Ibn Gabriol ~

The difference between average and top people can be explained in three words: And Then Some. They are thoughtful of others, they are considerate and kind – and then some. They meet their responsibilities and their obligations fairly and squarely – and then some. They are good friends to their friends and can be counted on in an emergency – and then some. ~ Mary Kay Ash ~

There are three types of people in the world: Those who make things happen, those who watch things happen, and those who wonder what happened. We all have a choice. You can decide which type of person you want to be. I have always chosen to be in the first group. ~ Mary Kay Ash ~

You truly are wonderful and when God created you. He had a beautiful and special plan for your life…He planted within you the seeds of greatness. You can be anything you want to be, you can climb any mountain you want to climb, and you can reach any goal you want to reach. It all lies within you. Believe in yourself. Have faith in yourself. Look for the best qualities in yourself. Believe that you are becoming the best you that you can be.
~ Mary Kay Ash ~

Be a dreamer. Have a sense of greatness. It has been said that if you can dream it, you can do it. And I believe it. Before your dream can become a reality, you have to see it in your own mind, see its fulfillment, whatever it may be. ~ Mary Kay Ash ~

I challenge you to think of each blessing as a burden and each burden as a blessing. ~ Mary Kay Ash ~

When you apply the Golden Rule and use your own good judgment along with a loving and caring spirit, you cannot go wrong. Your life will be enriched with friendships and blessings. ~ Mary Kay Ash ~

Don't turn your focus away from what is truly important. Instead, learn to evaluate your success by the balance you achieve in your life. ~ Mary Kay Ash ~

Never give up. Though many times adversity surrounds you, never give up! Success is just around the corner for the person who refuses to quit. ~ Mary Kay Ash ~

Having a plan to follow can provide you with an incredible source of power because it frees you from the exhaustion that results from having your thoughts and actions scattered.
~ And Then Some: Mary Kay ~

God didn't have time to create a nobody – just a somebody.
~ Mary Kay Ash ~

If it's to be, it's up to me. ~ Mary Kay Ash ~

Whatever you give away today or think or say or do will multiply about tenfold and then return to you. It may not come immediately nor from the obvious source, but the law applies unfailingly through some invisible force. Whatever you feel about another, be it love or hate or passion, will surely bounce right back to you in some clear or secret fashion. If you speak about some person, a word of praise or two, soon tens of other people will speak kind words to you. Our thoughts are broadcasts of the soul, not secrets of the brain. Kind ones bring us happiness, petty ones untold pain. Giving works as surely as reflections in a mirror. If hate you send, hate you'll get back, but loving brings love nearer. Remember as you start this day and duty crowds your mind, that kindness comes so quickly back to those who first are kind! Let that thought and this one direct you through the day…The only things we keep are the things we give away! ~ Mary Kay's Law of Life ~

You are confined only by the walls you build yourself.
~ Author unknown ~

You can close your eyes to what you do not want to see, but you can't close your heart to what you do not want to feel.
~ Johnny Depp ~

For you created my inmost being; you knit me together in my mother's womb. I praise you because I am fearfully and wonderfully made; your works are wonderful, I know that full well. My frame was not hidden from you when I was made in the secret place. When I was woven together in the depths of the earth, your eyes saw my unformed body. All the days ordained for me were written in your book before one of them came to be.
~ Psalm 139:13-16 ~

Your life is not determined by your circumstances but by your decisions. ~ Stephen Covey ~

Therefore, I tell you, do not worry about your life, what you will eat or drink, or about your body, what you will wear. Is not life more than food and the body more than clothes? Look at the birds of the air; they do not sow or reap or store away in barns, and yet your heavenly Father feeds them. Are you not much more valuable than they? Can any one of you by worrying add a single hour to your life? ~ Matthew 6:25-27 NIV ~

Now faith is being sure of what we hope for and certain of what we do not see. ~ Hebrew 11:1 NIV ~

Never base your life decisions on advice from people who don't have to deal with the results. ~ Author unknown ~

Each one should test their own actions they can take pride in themselves alone without comparing themselves to someone else. For each one should carry their own load. ~ Galatians 6:4-5 ~

As iron sharpens iron, so one man sharpens another.
~ Proverbs 27:17 NIV ~

You can't stop people from being who they are, but you can stop you from being who you are not. ~ Author unknown ~

Those who cannot remember the past are condemned to repeat it.
~ George Santayana ~

People don't care how much you know until they know how much you care. ~ John C. Maxwell ~

What is clear to you is clear to you. ~ Toni Cordell ~

While I move like a snail on valium, it is still forward.
~ Toni Cordell ~

Happiness is a club without dues or mission statement.
~ Glenn Proctor, Proctorisms ~

Technology has made vacations more traumatic than work."
~ Glenn Proctor, Proctorisms ~

Exercise, Eat Right, Get Sleep
~ Glenn Proctor, Proctorisms ~

Think EGO – Energy Gets Opportunity
~ Glenn Proctor, Proctorisms ~

Don't miss your bus. In this economy, there are few of them.
~ Glenn Proctor, Proctorisms ~

If you don't create your own direction, others will help you stay
lost. ~ Glenn Proctor, Proctorisms ~

Never say I wish – Say I did. Die with no regrets.
~ Glenn Proctor, Proctorisms ~

Push the plow in the right direction and the plow will share half the load. ~ Glenn Proctor, Proctorisms ~

"The thing to remember about the curves, turns, stops and starts of LIFE is that you're doing the driving."
~ Glenn Proctor, Proctorisms ~

The most ironic thing about life is that no one knows when they reach the middle. ~ Glenn Proctor, Proctorisms ~

Believe. Focus. Plan. Execute. ~ Glenn Proctor, Proctorisms ~

If you think the mountain is too high, then it is. Don't be upset when others climb over you. ~ Glenn Proctor, Proctorisms ~

Success has no color, age, gender or zip code. Find resilience without excuses. ~ Glenn Proctor, Proctorisms ~

Never lie to the face in the mirror. ~ Glenn Proctor, Proctorisms ~

Until your buzzer sounds, you have time for winning moments. ~ Glenn Proctor, Proctorisms ~

Opportunity dances with those already on the dance floor. ~ H. Jackson Brown, Jr. ~

Be still, and know that I am God. ~ Psalm 4:10 ~

Hope is the confident expectation that God will do what He said He's going to do. ~ Author unknown ~

God takes us from points of immaturity and infancy and pushes us into our purpose. ~ Reverend Victor Desmond Tate ~

When you have purpose, you move from a place of believing to a place of knowing. ~ Reverend Victor Desmond Tate ~

If you are going to fail, fail fast and keep it moving.
~ John Martin ~

You can't move forward moving backward.
~ Reverend Dwayne Harris ~

If you do what you have always done, you will always go where you have already been. ~ Author unknown ~

When I let go of what I am, I become what I might be.
~ Lao Tzu ~

Success is not final, failure is not fatal; it is the courage to continue that counts. ~ Winston Churchill ~

Ditch digging: The only job where the better you are at it, the lower you go. ~ Reverend Dr. Haywood Gray ~

You can't dig a ditch for someone else without getting dirt on yourself and you can slip and fall in the hole you dug.
~ Reverend Dr. Haywood Gray ~

Strive not to be a success but rather to be of value.
~ Albert Einstein ~

The most common way people give up their power is by thinking they don't have any. ~ Alice Walker ~

You miss 100% of the shots you don't take.
~ Wayne Gretzky ~

When I stand before God at the end of my life, I would hope that I would not have a single bit of talent left and could say, I used everything you gave me. ~ Erma Bombeck ~

Believe you can and you're halfway there.
~ Theodore Roosevelt ~

Let us not become weary in doing good, for at the proper time, we will reap a harvest if we do not give up.
~ Galatians 6:9 NIV ~

Trouble comes to everybody but misery is an option.
~ Author unknown ~

Now faith is the substance of things hoped for, the evidence of things not seen. ~ Hebrew 11:1 KJV ~

You can have a condition without the condition having you.
~ Author unknown ~

Success is measured not by the position one has reached in life as by obstacles which were overcome. ~ Booker T. Washington ~

And if one will hold on, he will discover that God walks with him and that God is able to lift you from the fatigue of despair to the buoyancy of hope, and transform dark and desolate valleys into sunlit paths of inner peace. ~ President Barack Obama ~

One doubt is the beginning of defeat. ~ Gerry Bayle ~

Whatever the mind of man can conceive and believe, it can achieve. ~ Napoleon Hill ~

Feel the fear and do it anyway.
~ Author unknown ~

Capture every day and be on purpose for the lives you want to impact. ~ National Sales Director Lady Crisette Ellis ~

The things we run away from are the very things we are supposed to do. The sad thing is waking up one day and you have not done what you were supposed to do and there's no time left.
~ National Sales Director Lady Crisette Ellis ~

If you show me your friends, I will show you your future.
~ Author unknown ~

Look down at your feet. If you don't do anything different, you will be in the same spot this time next year.
~ Author unknown ~

You become like the three people you hang around.
~ Author unknown ~

Authentically driven people neither avoid looking at their past nor do they stare in the rearview mirror. ~ Kim Honeycutt

If you don't believe you matter, the success you find will not matter. ~ Kim Honeycutt ~

You don't have to be great to start but you have to start to be great.
~ Zig Ziglar ~

If you want to go fast, go alone. If you want to go far, go together.
~ Author unknown ~

Be sure to take time to center yourself as each day comes. As you know, there's only one you, the moving and driving force of productivity. ~ Author unknown ~

When someone shows you how they are, proceed with caution; when they tell you how they are, listen and make a decision.
~ Pamela R. H. Lue-Hing ~

I cheated on my fears, broke up with my doubts, got engaged to my faith, and now I'm marrying my dreams. Soon, I will be holding hands with destiny!
~ Eddie A. Rios ~

For I know the plans I have for you, "declares the Lord," plans to prosper you and not to harm you, plans to give you hope and a future. ~ Jeremiah 29:11 ~

Do not conform to the pattern of this world, but be transformed by the renewing of your mind. ~ Romans 12:2 ~

The destiny of thousands is relying on the obedience of one. ~ Author unknown ~

For as he thinketh in his heart, so is he... ~ Proverbs 23:7 ~

Man is not the creature of circumstances; circumstances are the creatures of men. We are free agents, and man is more powerful than matter. ~ Benjamin Disraeli ~

Man is born to live and not to prepare to live. ~ Boris Pasternak ~

When someone is drowning, sometimes you have to allow them to go under a few times before they appreciate the air they're breathing. ~ Raphael Love ~

Achieve goals and learn the lessons with ease and grace.
~ Denise Cooper ~

Be happy with what you have while working on what you want.
~ Helen Keller ~

There is no elevator to the top. You have to take the stairs.
~ Steve Harvey ~

Life takes on meaning when you become motivated, set goals and charge after them in an unstoppable manner.
~ Les Brown ~

God has a purpose for your pain, a reason for your struggles and a reward for your faithfulness…don't give up!
~ Author unknown ~

If you ever want your soul to dance in the clouds, you will at some point have to juggle lightning and taste the thunder.
~ Christopher Poindexter ~

Each decision we make, each action we take, is born out of an intention. ~ Sharon Salzberg ~

There's nothing magical about people who have gone from no money to $1 million or $20 million – they were just crazy enough to put themselves out there. ~ Tabatha Turman ~

And the day came when the risk to remain tight in a bud was more painful than the risk it took to blossom. ~ Anais Nin ~

Happiness is when what you think, what you say, and what you do are in harmony. ~ Mahatma Gandhi ~

High achievement always takes place in the framework of high expectation. ~ Charles Kettering, Inventor ~

A leader takes people where they want to go. A great leader takes people where they don't necessarily want to go, but ought to be. ~ Rosalynn Carter ~

Out of intense complexities, intense simplicities emerge. ~ Winston Churchill ~

Only those who dare to fail greatly can ever achieve greatly. ~ Author unknown ~

Where do you find diamonds? Deep down in the ground, covered and protected. Where do you find pearls? Deep down at the bottom of the ocean, covered up and protected in a beautiful shell. Where do you find gold? Way down in the mine, covered over with layers of rock and to get them, you have to work hard and dig deep down to get them. Moral of the story: You are far more precious than gold, diamonds and pearls…you are worth it…dig deep. ~ Author Unknown ~

Do the best you can until you know better. Then when you know better, do better. ~ Maya Angelou ~

A river cuts through rock, not because of its power, but because of its persistence. ~ Jim Watkins ~

Don't raise your voice, improve your argument.
~ Bishop Desmond Tutu ~

You attract the right things when you have a sense of who you are.
~ Amy Poehler ~

The most confused we ever get is when we try to convince our heads of something our hearts know is a lie.
~ Karen Moning ~

Nobody can go back and start a new beginning, but anyone can start today and make a new ending. ~ Maria Robinson ~

Three things you cannot recover in life: The word after it's said; the moment after it's missed; and the time after it's gone.
~ Inspower ~

If you can't fly, then run; if you can't run, then walk; if you can't walk, then crawl, but whatever you do, you have to keep moving forward. ~ Dr. Martin Luther King ~

It's not what happens to you that matters. It's how you respond to what happens to you that makes a difference. ~ Zig Ziglar ~

I'm convinced that about half of what separates the successful entrepreneurs from the non-successful ones is pure perseverance. ~ Steve Jobs ~

To trust others one must first trust self. In other words, one must value their own integrity, character qualities as well as possess a strong confidence in one's self. ~ Author unknown ~

In order to take the next step, you have to let other great people flock together with you without being intimidated by their greatness! Truly great people can accommodate the greatness of others, only insecure people have to shoot down every other great person in order to function because their fear is that if people see options, they will be excluded. Don't be great by yourself! ~ T. D. Jakes ~

We make a living by what we get, but we make a life by what we give. ~ Winston Churchill ~

Perfection is not attainable, but if we chase perfection we can catch excellence. ~ Vince Lombardi ~

Everyone thinks of changing the world, but no one thinks of changing himself. ~ Leo Tolstoy ~

If you're brave enough to say goodbye, life will reward you with a new hello. ~ Author unknown ~

I believe anything is possible. I see opportunity when others see impossibility. I take risks. I'm focused. I hustle. I know that nothing is unrealistic. I feel overwhelming love. I embrace my childlike wonder and curiosity. I take flying leaps into the unknown. I contribute to something bigger than myself. I create. I learn. I grow. I do. I believe it's never too late to start living a dream. I am an entrepreneur. ~ Author unknown ~

The ultimate measure of a man is not where he stands in moments of comfort and convenience, but where he stands at times of challenge and controversy.
~ Dr. Martin Luther King, Jr. ~

Forgiveness is not an occasional act. It is a permanent attitude.
~ Dr. Martin Luther King, Jr. ~

Faith is taking the first step even when you don't see the whole staircase. ~ Dr. Martin Luther King, Jr. ~

Life's most persistent and urgent question is, "What are you doing for others?" ~ Dr. Martin Luther King, Jr. ~

Our lives begin to end the day we become silent about things that matter. ~ Dr. Martin Luther King, Jr. ~

Change does not roll in on the wheels of inevitability, but comes through continuous struggle. ~ Dr. Martin Luther King, Jr. ~

Love is the only force capable of transforming an enemy into friend. ~ Dr. Martin Luther King, Jr. ~

If a man is called to be a street sweeper, he should sweep streets even as Michelangelo painted, or Beethoven composed music, or Shakespeare wrote poetry. He should sweep streets so well that all the hosts of heaven and earth will pause to say, "Here lived a great street sweeper who did his job well."
~ Dr. Martin Luther King, Jr. ~

Success is no accident. It is hard work, perseverance, learning, studying, sacrifice and most of all, love of what you are doing.
~ Pele ~

Life is 10% what happens to us and 90% how we react to it.
~ Dennis Kimbro ~

There is no royal road to anything. One thing at a time, all things in succession. That which grows fast, withers as rapidly. That which grows slowly, endures.
~ Josiah Gilbert Holland ~

Even if you're on the right track, you'll get run over if you just sit there. ~ Will Rogers ~

Courage is the first of human qualities because it is the quality which guarantees all others. ~ Winston Churchill ~

The great thing in this world is not so much where you stand, as in what direction you are moving. ~ Oliver Wendell Holmes ~

Live each day as if your life had just begun.
~ Johann Wolfgang Von Goethe ~

Either you run the day or the day runs you.
~ Jim Rohn ~

I don't know the key to success, but the key to failure is trying to please everybody. ~ Bill Cosby ~

Do not let what you cannot do interfere with what you can do.
~John Wooden~

Challenges are what make life interesting and overcoming them is what makes life meaningful. ~ Joshua J. Marine ~

Every strike brings me closer to the next home run.
~ Babe Ruth ~

We become what we think about. ~ Earl Nightingale ~

Eighty percent of success is showing up. ~ Woody Allen ~

Keep away from people who try to belittle your ambitions. Small people always do that, but the really great makes you feel that you, too, can become great. ~ Mark Twain ~

I am not a product of my circumstances; I am a product of my decisions. ~ Stephen Covey ~

An obstacle is often a stepping stone. ~ Prescott ~

The rest revenge is massive success. ~ Frank Sinatra ~

The journey of a thousand miles begins with one step.
~ Lao Tzu ~

Life is really simple, but we insist on making it complicated.
~ Confucius ~

In the end, it's not the years in your life that count. It's the life in your years. ~ Abraham Lincoln ~

For beautiful eyes, look for the good in others; for beautiful lips, speak only words of kindness; and for poise, walk with the knowledge that you are never alone. ~ Audrey Hepburn ~

Do not go where the path may lead, go instead where there is no path and leave a trail. ~ Ralph Waldo Emerson ~

Vision without action is just a dream. Action without a vision is merely a passing of time, but a vision with action can change the world. ~ Author unknown ~

FOCUS: Follow One Course Until Successful.
~ Author unknown ~

There's greatness in you, you simply must believe it.
~ Author unknown ~

The longer I live, the more I realize the impact of attitude on life. Attitude, to me, is more important than facts. It is more important than the past, than education, than money, than circumstances, than failures, than successes, than what other people think or say or do. It is more important than appearance, giftedness, or skill. It will make or break a company...a church...a home. The remarkable thing is we have a choice every day regarding the attitude we will embrace for that day. We cannot change our past...we cannot change the fact that people will act in a certain way. We cannot change the inevitable. The only thing we can do is play on the one string we have, and that is our attitude...I am convinced that life is 10% what happens to me and 90% how I react to it.
~ Charles Swindoll ~

7 P's: Prior Proper Planning Prevents Pitifully Poor Performance.
~ Author unknown ~

...Much will be required from everyone to whom much has been given. But even more will be demanded from the one to whom much has been entrusted. ~ Luke 12:48 ISV

Envision the win within ~ Pamela R. H. Lue-Hing ~

Education is the passport to the future, for tomorrow belongs to those who prepare for it today. ~ Malcolm X ~

It's not the height of the mountain that matters, but you're determination to make the climb.
~ Author unknown ~

Success is to be measured not so much by the position that one has reached in life as by the obstacles which he has overcome.
~ Booker T. Washington ~

Love is like a virus, it can happen to anybody at any time.
~ Maya Angelou

There is no greater agony than bearing an untold story inside of you. ~ Maya Angelou ~

We delight in the beauty of the butterfly, but rarely admit the changes it has gone through to achieve that beauty.
~ Maya Angelou ~

Courage is the most important of all virtues because without courage, you can't practice any other virtue consistently.
~ Maya Angelou ~

My mission in life is not merely to survive, but to thrive; and to do so with some passion, some compassion, some humor, and some style. ~ Maya Angelou ~

Never make someone a priority when all you are to them is an option. ~ Maya Angelou ~

Try to be a rainbow in someone's cloud. ~ Maya Angelou ~

Ask for what you want and be prepared to get it!
~ Maya Angelou ~

Efforts and courage are not enough without purpose and direction.
~ President John F. Kennedy ~

Two roads diverged in a wood, and I – I took the one less traveled by, and that has made all the difference. ~ Robert Frost ~

Definiteness of purpose is the starting point of all achievement.
~ W. Clement Stone ~

An unexamined life is not worth living. ~ Socrates ~

Your time is limited, so don't waste it living someone else's life.
~ Steve Jobs ~

Winning isn't everything, but wanting to win is.
~ Vince Lombardi ~

You can never cross the ocean until you have the courage to lose
sight of the shore. ~ Christopher Columbus ~

The two most important days in your life are the day you are born
and the day you find out why. ~ Mark Twain ~

Our deepest fear is not that we are inadequate. Our deepest fear is
that we are powerful beyond measure. It is our light, not our
darkness that most frightens us. We ask ourselves, "Who am I to
be brilliant, gorgeous, talented, and fabulous?" Actually, who are
you not to be? You are a child of God. Your playing small does
not serve the world. There is nothing enlightened about shrinking
so that other people won't feel insecure around you. We are all
meant to shine, as children do. We were born to make manifest the
glory of God that is within us. It's not just in some of us; it's in
everyone. And as we let our own light shine, we unconsciously
give other people permission to do the same. As we are liberated
from our own fear, our presence automatically liberates others.
~ Marianne Williamson ~

Start where you are. Use what you have. Do what you can.
~ Arthur Ashe ~

People often say that motivation doesn't last. Well, neither does bathing. That's why we recommend it daily. ~ Zig Ziglar ~

Ask and it will be given to you; search, and you will find; knock and the door will be opened to you.
~ Jesus ~

About the Author

Pamela is the founder, CEO and strategic consultant of Legacy Partners, LLC. She is an author, speaker and coach who equips, educates and inspires people to move from employee to employer. For the last 20 years, she has focused on developing people, programs and businesses.

She has over 30 years in strategic planning, Sales and Marketing, and a wealth of knowledge as an enterprising entrepreneur. As a strategic business and sales consultant, she draws upon her knowledge as a Board Certified Life Coach and Human Behavior Consultant to bring a "whole" new meaning to doing business.

Community engagement is her passion. In her spare time, she volunteers with the Young Black Men's Leadership Alliance, moderates Mecklenburg County Commissioner Vilma D. Leake's bi-monthly Small Business Consortium meetings, and previously served on the Small Business and Entrepreneurship Advisory Board for Mecklenburg County in Charlotte, North Carolina.

As a keynote speaker, moderator, workshop and seminar facilitator, she connects with the audience and brings subject matter to life. Pamela is best known for her ingenuity in building something from nothing and her uncanny ability to see the big picture as well as the small details. Her "no non-sense, methodical, make-it-happen" style takes clients from where they are to where they want to be.

Note from the Author

Please visit my website at **www.pamelaluehing.com** to learn about my other products and leave a comment:

Pink Slip to POWERHOUSE: 12 Steps to Next

Pink Slip to POWERHOUSE: 12 Steps to Next Workbook

Pink Slip to POWERHOUSE: 12 Steps to Next 90 Day Journal

Powerhouse Bootcamp

If you are interested in a complimentary coaching or consultative session, complete the contact form via the website or call (800) 975-9624.

Yours in Success!

Pamela

www.ingramcontent.com/pod-product-compliance
Lightning Source LLC
Chambersburg PA
CBHW071939020426
42331CB00010B/2933